I-C-E

In Case *of* Emergency

Your Essential Medical Journal

MAUREEN ROONEY GILBERT

BALBOA.
PRESS

A DIVISION OF HAY HOUSE

Balboa Press books may be ordered through booksellers or by contacting:

Balboa Press
A Division of Hay House
1663 Liberty Drive
Bloomington, IN 47403
www.balboapress.com
1 (877) 407-4847

Print information available on the last page.

ISBN: 978-1-5043-7960-1 (sc)
ISBN: 978-1-5043-7987-8 (e)

Library of Congress Control Number: 2017906518

Balboa Press rev. date: 07/19/2017

IN CASE OF AN
EMERGENCY
DIAL 911
IMMEDIATELY

TRIBUTE

I would be remiss if I did not take this opportunity to thank, honor and celebrate all first responders. An article published by the Department of Homeland Security First Responder Commercialization reports there are over 25,000,000 first responders in the US.

Whether you're police or fire personnel, an EMT or medical staff at a hospital, you perform an absolutely critical and necessary need. In times of tragedy, you've shown us, again and again, you know no boundaries. You are quick to answer the call of duty anywhere at any time. For that, we thank you. I believe this quote from Mother Teresa applies to all first responders: "We can do no great things; only small things with great love." I salute you for your selfless acts of service and professionalism.

"NEXT TO CREATING A LIFE, THE FINEST
THING A MAN CAN DO IS SAVE ONE."
ABRAHAM LINCOLN

**You think you're having a heart attack.
There's been a car accident.
Your child is having a life threatening asthma attack.
You have gone into pre-mature labor.**

Few of us ever expect to find ourselves in need of emergency medical care. But when we do, time is of the essence. So it's crucial to make each minute count. All medical emergencies can be terrifying for you, as the patient, your family, friends and care takers. Statistics provided by the Journal of Emergency Medical Services, report that over 36,700,000 calls annually are received by first responders alerting them of potential emergencies.

In the event you require emergency medical care, it is imperative first responders are provided with accurate, up to date and complete health history to best provide you with effective and safe emergency care. There is a medical phenomenon known to first responders as the "golden hour" which refers to a trauma victim's greatest chance of survival being within the first hour.

Everyone wants to be involved in the decision making process regarding their own healthcare. But, unfortunately, in times of such emergencies, the stress, anxiety or one's inability to communicate, can hamper a person's ability to relate the necessary information first responders need for their initial assessment and course of action. I-C-E, In Case of Emergency, can be that tool that assists you in being as involved as possible.

This book is designed to provide all first responders, including the hospital staff, with your medical history so you receive the best care and eliminate potentially costly, or even deadly, mistakes caused by incomplete or incorrect information.

For this book, I-C-E, In Case of Emergency, to be most effective, keep one in a designated place in your home, in the glove compartment of your car and your children's backpack. God forbid, should an emergency occur on their way to school or an after school event, then the necessary information is readily available to first responders and hospital staff.

This book is for your benefit. Use it for your benefit however that may look for you personally.

It is also a useful and practical tool to take to routine doctor appointments to ensure your medical chart is kept current and accurate with medicines and procedures.

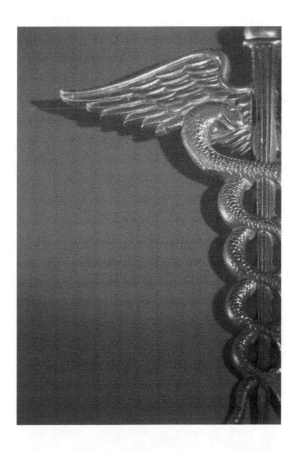

PERSONAL MEDICAL STATS

NAME _____ D/O/B _____

ADDRESS _____

BLOOD TYPE _____ WEIGHT _____

BLOOD PRESSURE _____ PREFERRED LANGUAGE _____

ORGAN/TISSUE DONOR _____

ANY DISABILITY THAT WOULD AFFECT COMMUNICATING
WITH FIRST RESPONDERS? _____

_____

HISTORY OF RECREATIONAL DRUGS _____

TYPES OF DRUGS _____

ALCOHOL USE _____ CONSUMPTION _____

TOBACCO HISTORY _____

NOTES

_____

_____

_____

_____'S
I – C – E CONTACTS

NAME _____ PHONE _____

RELATIONSHIP _____

NAME _____ PHONE _____

RELATIONSHIP _____

NAME _____ PHONE _____

RELATIONSHIP _____

NAME _____ PHONE _____

RELATIONSHIP _____

NAME _____ PHONE _____

RELATIONSHIP _____

_____'S

CRITICAL AND LIFE THREATENING CONDITIONS

ALLERGY	MEDICAL ISSUE	REACTION	ANTIDOTE

NOTES

_____

_____

_____

_____

_____

_____'S

INSURANCE INFORMATION

PRIMARY INSURANCE _____

POLICY HOLDER _____

GROUP # _____ ID # _____

LAST 4 SS# DIGITS _____

SECONDARY INSURANCE _____

POLICY HOLDER _____

GROUP # _____ ID # _____

_____'s PREFERRED HOSPITAL _____

Preferred hospital may be an issue whether it is in network with your primary or secondary insurance. Stating a "preferred" hospital does not guarantee first responders will be able to honor your preference. They will make that decision based on many factors such as the hospital best suited to your medical emergency.

_____'s RELIGIOUS AFFILIATION _____

Religious affiliation is an important issue for those of a faith that limits or prohibits medical treatments such as blood transfusions.

_____'S
DOCTOR'S CONTACT INFORMATION

PRIMARY _____

PHONE _____

ADDRESS _____

SPECIALIST _____

PHONE _____

ADDRESS _____

SPECIALIST _____

PHONE _____

ADDRESS _____

SPECIALIST _____

PHONE _____

ADDRESS _____

SPECIALIST _____

PHONE _____

ADDRESS _____

_____'S
PERSONAL MEDICAL CHART

MEDICATIONS PRESCRIPTIONS & OTC AND DOSES	TREATMENT	HEALTH CARE PROFESSIONAL	PHONE

_____'S
HOSPITALIZATION CHART

REASON FOR HOSPITALIZATION	DATE	TREATMENT	COMPLICATIONS

NOTES

_____

_____

_____

_____

_____

_____'S
SURGERY CHART

PROCEDURE	DATE	TREATMENT	COMPLICATIONS

NOTES

_____

_____

_____

_____

_____

_____'S

ALLERGIES, SENSITIVITIES AND REACTIONS
(Non-Life Threatening Conditions)

MEDICINE	FOOD	OTC and/or SUPPLEMENTS	COMPLICATIONS

NOTES

_____

_____

_____

_____

_____

_____'S
LEGAL INFORMATION

ATTORNEY _____

PHONE _____

LIVING WILL YES _____ NO _____

LOCATION _____

DURABLE POWER OF ATTORNEY YES _____ NO _____

LOCATION _____

APPOINTED PERSON _____

_____

_____

NOTES

_____

_____

_____

_____

_____

_____'S

END OF LIFE MEDICAL DECISIONS

It should be understood I am to be consulted and actively involved, to the fullest of my ability, in the decision making process of all life sustaining measures, as well as the discontinuation of all life sustaining measures, as long as I am deemed mentally competent as defined by the State I reside, as determined by two (2) attending physicians.

If at some point in time I no longer meet the definition for mental competency by the State in which I reside as determined by 2 licensed attending physicians, I appoint one of the following people, listed in said order, the authority to make life termination decisions on my behalf:

NAME _____ PHONE _____

RELATIONSHIP _____

NAME _____ PHONE _____

RELATIONSHIP _____

NAME _____ PHONE _____

RELATIONSHIP _____

Must Initial and date page:

_____

_____'S
FUNERAL WISHES

MEMORIAL SERVICE YES _____ No _____

LOCATION _____

_____

CREMATION YES _____ NO _____

PLACE OF INTERNMENT _____

NOTES

_____

_____

_____

_____

_____

EVERYDAY HEROES

PERSONAL MEDICAL STATS

NAME _____ D/O/B _____

ADDRESS _____

BLOOD TYPE _____ WEIGHT _____

BLOOD PRESSURE _____ PREFERRED LANGUAGE _____

ORGAN/TISSUE DONOR _____

ANY DISABILITY THAT WOULD AFFECT COMMUNICATING
WITH FIRST RESPONDERS? _____

_____

HISTORY OF RECREATIONAL DRUGS _____

TYPES OF DRUGS _____

ALCOHOL USE _____ CONSUMPTION _____

TOBACCO HISTORY _____

NOTES

_____

_____

_____

_____'S
I – C – E CONTACTS

NAME _____ PHONE _____

RELATIONSHIP_____

NAME _____ PHONE _____

RELATIONSHIP_____

NAME _____ PHONE _____

RELATIONSHIP_____

NAME _____ PHONE _____

RELATIONSHIP _____

NAME _____ PHONE _____

RELATIONSHIP _____

_____'S
CRITICAL AND LIFE THREATENING CONDITIONS

ALLERGY	MEDICAL ISSUE	REACTION	ANTIDOTE

NOTES

_____

_____

_____

_____

_____

_____'S
INSURANCE INFORMATION

PRIMARY INSURANCE _____

POLICY HOLDER _____

GROUP # _____ ID # _____

LAST 4 SS# DIGITS _____

SECONDARY INSURANCE _____

POLICY HOLDER _____

GROUP # _____ ID # _____

_____'s PREFERRED HOSPITAL _____

Preferred hospital may be an issue whether it is in network with your primary or secondary insurance. Stating a "preferred" hospital does not guarantee first responders will be able to honor your preference. They will make that decision based on many factors such as the hospital best suited to your medical emergency.

_____'s RELIGIOUS AFFILIATION _____

Religious affiliation is an important issue for those of a faith that limits or prohibits medical treatments such as blood transfusions.

_____'S
DOCTOR'S CONTACT INFORMATION

PRIMARY _____

PHONE _____

ADDRESS _____

SPECIALIST _____

PHONE _____

ADDRESS _____

SPECIALIST _____

PHONE _____

ADDRESS _____

SPECIALIST _____

PHONE _____

ADDRESS _____

SPECIALIST _____

PHONE _____

ADDRESS _____

_____'S

PERSONAL MEDICAL CHART

MEDICATIONS PRESCRIPTIONS & OTC AND DOSES	TREATMENT	HEALTH CARE PROFESSIONAL	PHONE

_____'S

HOSPITALIZATION CHART

REASON FOR HOSPITALIZATION	DATE	TREATMENT	COMPLICATIONS

NOTES

_____

_____

_____

_____

_____

_____'S

SURGERY CHART

PROCEDURE	DATE	TREATMENT	COMPLICATIONS

NOTES

_____

_____

_____

_____

_____

_____'S

ALLERGIES, SENSITIVITIES AND REACTIONS
(Non-Life Threatening Conditions)

MEDICINE	FOOD	OTC and/or SUPPLEMENTS	COMPLICATIONS

NOTES

_____

_____

_____

_____

_____'S

LEGAL INFORMATION

ATTORNEY _____

PHONE _____

LIVING WILL YES _____ NO _____

LOCATION _____

DURABLE POWER OF ATTORNEY YES _____ NO _____

LOCATION _____

APPOINTED PERSON _____

_____

_____

NOTES

_____

_____

_____

_____

_____

_____'S
END OF LIFE MEDICAL DECISIONS

It should be understood I am to be consulted and actively involved, to the fullest of my ability, in the decision making process of all life sustaining measures, as well as the discontinuation of all life sustaining measures, as long as I am deemed mentally competent as defined by the State I reside, as determined by two (2) attending physicians.

If at some point in time I no longer meet the definition for mental competency by the State in which I reside as determined by 2 licensed attending physicians, I appoint one of the following people, listed in said order, the authority to make life termination decisions on my behalf:

NAME _____ PHONE _____

RELATIONSHIP _____

NAME _____ PHONE _____

RELATIONSHIP _____

NAME _____ PHONE _____

RELATIONSHIP _____

Must Initial and date page:

_____

_____'S
FUNERAL WISHES

MEMORIAL SERVICE YES _____ No _____

LOCATION _____

_____

CREMATION YES _____ NO _____

PLACE OF INTERNMENT _____

NOTES

_____

_____

_____

_____

_____

EVERYDAY HEROES

CHILD'S MEDICAL STATS

NAME _____ D/O/B _____

ADDRESS _____

BLOOD TYPE _____ WEIGHT _____

PREFERRED LANGUAGE _____

ORGAN/TISSUE DONOR _____

HISTORY OF RECREATIONAL DRUGS _____

TYPES OF DRUGS _____

ALCOHOL USE _____ CONSUMPTION _____

TOBACCO HISTORY _____

ANY DISABILITY THAT WOULD AFFECT COMMUNICATING
WITH FIRST RESPONDERS? _____

_____

MOTHER'S FULL NAME _____

LAST 4 DIGITS OF SS# _____

FATHER'S FULL NAME _____

LAST 4 DIGITS OF SS# _____

_____'S

I – C – E CONTACTS

NAME _____ PHONE _____

RELATIONSHIP _____

NAME _____ PHONE _____

RELATIONSHIP _____

NAME _____ PHONE _____

RELATIONSHIP _____

NAME _____ PHONE _____

RELATIONSHIP _____

NAME _____ PHONE _____

RELATIONSHIP _____

_____'S

CRITICAL AND LIFE THREATENING CONDITIONS

ALLERGY	MEDICAL ISSUE	REACTION	ANTIDOTE

NOTES

_____

_____

_____

_____

_____

_____'S

CHILDHOOD VACCINATION CHART

VACCINE	1ST DOSE	2ND DOSE	3RD DOSE	4TH DOSE	5TH DOSE
HEPATITIS A					
HEPATITIS B					
DTaP					
MMR					
PCV					
IPV					

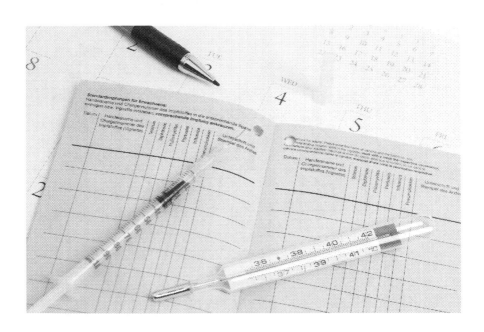

_____'S
INSURANCE INFORMATION

PRIMARY INSURANCE _____

POLICY HOLDER _____

GROUP # _____ ID # _____

SECONDARY INSURANCE _____

POLICY HOLDER _____

GROUP # _____ ID # _____

_____'s PREFERRED HOSPITAL _____

Preferred hospital may be an issue whether it is in network with your primary or secondary insurance. Stating a "preferred" hospital does not guarantee first responders will be able to honor your preference. They will make that decision based on many factors such as the hospital best suited to your medical emergency.

_____'s RELIGIOUS AFFILIATION _____

Religious affiliation is an important issue for those of a faith that limits or prohibits medical treatments such as blood transfusions.

_____'S

DOCTOR'S CONTACT INFORMATION

PRIMARY _____

PHONE _____

ADDRESS _____

SPECIALIST _____

PHONE _____

ADDRESS _____

SPECIALIST _____

PHONE _____

ADDRESS _____

SPECIALIST _____

PHONE _____

ADDRESS _____

SPECIALIST _____

PHONE _____

ADDRESS _____

_____'S

PERSONAL MEDICAL CHART

MEDICATIONS PRESCRIPTIONS & OTC AND DOSES	TREATMENT	HEALTH CARE PROFESSIONAL	PHONE

_____'S
HOSPITALIZATION CHART

REASON FOR HOSPITALIZATION	DATE	TREATMENT	COMPLICATIONS

NOTES

_____

_____

_____

_____

_____

_____'S
SURGERY CHART

PROCEDURE	DATE	TREATMENT	COMPLICATIONS

NOTES

_____

_____

_____

_____

_____

_____'S

ALLERGIES, SENSITIVITIES AND REACTIONS
(Non-Life Threatening Conditions)

MEDICINE	FOOD	OTC and/or SUPPLEMENTS	COMPLICATIONS

NOTES

_____

_____

_____

_____

_____'S
LEGAL INFORMATION

ATTORNEY _____

PHONE _____

LIVING WILL YES _____ NO _____

LOCATION _____

DURABLE POWER OF ATTORNEY YES _____ NO _____

LOCATION _____

APPOINTED PERSON _____

_____

_____

NOTES

_____

_____

_____

_____

_____

_____'s

END OF LIFE MEDICAL DECISIONS

It should be understood I am to be consulted and actively involved, to the fullest of my ability, in the decision making process of all life sustaining measures, as well as the discontinuation of all life sustaining measures, as long as I am deemed mentally competent as defined by the State I reside, as determined by two (2) attending physicians.

If at some point in time I no longer meet the definition for mental competency by the State in which I reside as determined by 2 licensed attending physicians, I appoint one of the following people, listed in said order, the authority to make life termination decisions on my behalf:

NAME _____ PHONE _____

RELATIONSHIP _____

NAME _____ PHONE _____

RELATIONSHIP _____

NAME _____ PHONE _____

RELATIONSHIP _____

Must Initial and date page:

_____

_____'S
FUNERAL WISHES

MEMORIAL SERVICE YES _____ No _____

LOCATION _____

_____

CREMATION YES _____ NO _____

PLACE OF INTERNMENT _____

NOTES

_____

_____

_____

_____

_____

EVERYDAY HERO

CHILD'S MEDICAL STATS

NAME _____ D/O/B _____

ADDRESS _____

BLOOD TYPE _____ WEIGHT _____

PREFERRED LANGUAGE _____

ORGAN/TISSUE DONOR _____

HISTORY OF RECREATIONAL DRUGS _____

TYPES OF DRUGS _____

ALCOHOL USE _____ CONSUMPTION _____

TOBACCO HISTORY _____

ANY DISABILITY THAT WOULD AFFECT COMMUNICATING
WITH FIRST RESPONDERS? _____

_____

MOTHER'S FULL NAME _____

LAST 4 DIGITS OF SS# _____

FATHER'S FULL NAME _____

LAST 4 DIGITS OF SS# _____

_____'S
I – C – E CONTACTS

NAME _____ PHONE _____

RELATIONSHIP _____

NAME _____ PHONE _____

RELATIONSHIP _____

NAME _____ PHONE _____

RELATIONSHIP _____

NAME _____ PHONE _____

RELATIONSHIP _____

NAME _____ PHONE _____

RELATIONSHIP _____

_____'S

CRITICAL AND LIFE THREATHENING CONDITIONS

ALLERGY	MEDICAL ISSUE	REACTION	ANTIDOTE

NOTES

_____

_____

_____

_____

_____

_____'S

CHILDHOOD VACCINATION CHART

VACCINE	1ST DOSE	2ND DOSE	3RD DOSE	4TH DOSE	5TH DOSE
HEPATITIS A					
HEPATITIS B					
DTaP					
MMR					
PCV					
IPV					

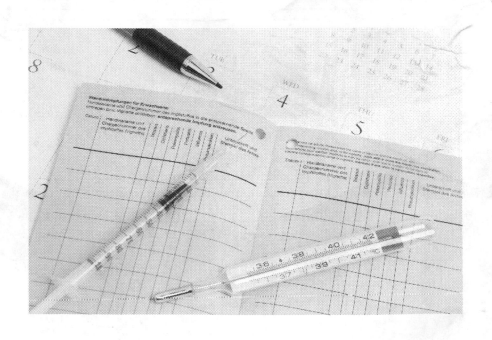

_____'S

INSURANCE INFORMATION

PRIMARY INSURANCE _____

POLICY HOLDER _____

GROUP # _____ ID # _____

SECONDARY INSURANCE _____

POLICY HOLDER _____

GROUP # _____ ID # _____

_____'s PREFERRED HOSPITAL _____

Preferred hospital may be an issue whether it is in network with
your primary or secondary insurance. Stating a "preferred"
hospital does not guarantee first responders will be able to honor
your preference. They will make that decision based on many
factors such as the hospital best suited to your medical emergency.

_____'s RELIGIOUS AFFILIATION _____

Religious affiliation is an important issue for those of a faith that
limits or prohibits medical treatments such as blood transfusions.

_____'S

DOCTOR'S CONTACT INFORMATION

PRIMARY _____

PHONE _____

ADDRESS _____

SPECIALIST _____

PHONE _____

ADDRESS _____

SPECIALIST _____

PHONE _____

ADDRESS _____

SPECIALIST _____

PHONE _____

ADDRESS _____

SPECIALIST _____

PHONE _____

ADDRESS _____

_____'S
PERSONAL MEDICAL CHART

MEDICATIONS PRESCRIPTIONS & OTC AND DOSES	TREATMENT	HEALTH CARE PROFESSIONAL	PHONE

_____'S
HOSPITALIZATION CHART

REASON FOR HOSPITALIZATION	DATE	TREATMENT	COMPLICATIONS

NOTES

_____

_____

_____

_____

_____

_____'S
SURGERY CHART

PROCEDURE	DATE	TREATMENT	COMPLICATIONS

NOTES

_____

_____

_____

_____

_____

_____'S

ALLERGIES, SENSITIVITIES AND REACTIONS
(Non-Life Threatening Conditions)

MEDICINE	FOOD	OTC and/or SUPPLEMENTS	COMPLICATIONS

NOTES

_____

_____

_____

_____

_____

_____'S
LEGAL INFORMATION

ATTORNEY _____

PHONE _____

LIVING WILL YES _____ NO _____

LOCATION _____

DURABLE POWER OF ATTORNEY YES _____ NO _____

LOCATION _____

APPOINTED PERSON _____

_____

_____

NOTES

_____

_____

_____

_____

_____

_____'S
END OF LIFE MEDICAL DECISIONS

It should be understood I am to be consulted and actively involved, to the fullest of my ability, in the decision making process of all life sustaining measures, as well as the discontinuation of all life sustaining measures, as long as I am deemed mentally competent as defined by the State I reside, as determined by two (2) attending physicians.

If at some point in time I no longer meet the definition for mental competency by the State in which I reside as determined by 2 licensed attending physicians, I appoint one of the following people, listed in said order, the authority to make life termination decisions on my behalf:

NAME _____ PHONE _____

RELATIONSHIP _____

NAME _____ PHONE _____

RELATIONSHIP _____

NAME _____ PHONE _____

RELATIONSHIP _____

Must Initial and date page:

_____

_____'S
FUNERAL WISHES

MEMORIAL SERVICE YES _____ No _____

LOCATION _____

_____

CREMATION YES _____ NO _____

PLACE OF INTERNMENT _____

NOTES

_____

_____

_____

_____

_____

EVERYDAY HEROES

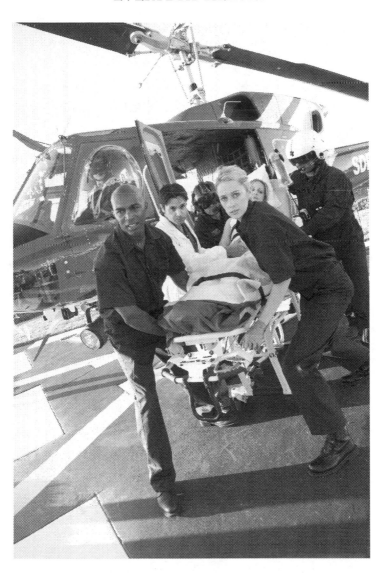

CHILD'S MEDICAL STATS

NAME _____ D/O/B _____

ADDRESS _____

BLOOD TYPE _____ WEIGHT _____

PREFERRED LANGUAGE _____

ORGAN/TISSUE DONOR _____

HISTORY OF RECREATIONAL DRUGS _____

TYPES OF DRUGS _____

ALCOHOL USE _____ CONSUMPTION _____

TOBACCO HISTORY _____

ANY DISABILITY THAT WOULD AFFECT COMMUNICATING
WITH FIRST RESPONDERS? _____

_____

MOTHER'S FULL NAME _____

LAST 4 DIGITS OF SS# _____

FATHER'S FULL NAME _____

LAST 4 DIGITS OF SS# _____

_____'S
I – C – E CONTACTS

NAME _____ PHONE _____

RELATIONSHIP _____

NAME _____ PHONE _____

RELATIONSHIP _____

NAME _____ PHONE _____

RELATIONSHIP _____

NAME _____ PHONE _____

RELATIONSHIP _____

NAME _____ PHONE _____

RELATIONSHIP _____

_____'S
CRITICAL AND LIFE THREATENING CONDITIONS

ALLERGY	MEDICAL ISSUE	REACTION	ANTIDOTE

NOTES

_____

_____

_____

_____

_____

_____'S

CHILDHOOD VACCINATION CHART

VACCINE	1ST DOSE	2ND DOSE	3RD DOSE	4TH DOSE	5TH DOSE
HEPATITIS A					
HEPATITIS B					
DTaP					
MMR					
PCV					
IPV					

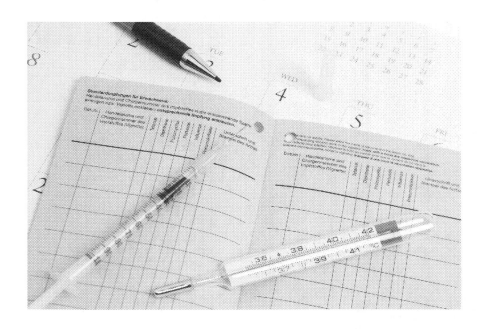

_____'S

INSURANCE INFORMATION

PRIMARY INSURANCE _____

POLICY HOLDER _____

GROUP # _____ ID # _____

SECONDARY INSURANCE _____

POLICY HOLDER _____

GROUP # _____ ID # _____

_____'s PREFERRED HOSPITAL _____

Preferred hospital may be an issue whether it is in network with your primary or secondary insurance. Stating a "preferred" hospital does not guarantee first responders will be able to honor your preference. They will make that decision based on many factors such as the hospital best suited to your medical emergency.

_____'s RELIGIOUS AFFILIATION _____

Religious affiliation is an important issue for those of a faith that limits or prohibits medical treatments such as blood transfusions.

_____'S

DOCTOR'S CONTACT INFORMATION

PRIMARY _____

PHONE _____

ADDRESS _____

SPECIALIST _____

PHONE _____

ADDRESS _____

SPECIALIST _____

PHONE _____

ADDRESS _____

SPECIALIST _____

PHONE _____

ADDRESS _____

SPECIALIST _____

PHONE _____

ADDRESS _____

_____'S

PERSONAL MEDICAL CHART

MEDICATIONS PRESCRIPTIONS & OTC AND DOSES	TREATMENT	HEALTH CARE PROFESSIONAL	PHONE

_____'S

HOSPITALIZATION CHART

REASON FOR HOSPITALIZATION	DATE	TREATMENT	COMPLICATIONS

NOTES

_____

_____

_____

_____

_____

_____'S
SURGERY CHART

PROCEDURE	DATE	TREATMENT	COMPLICATIONS

NOTES

_____

_____

_____

_____

_____

_____'S

ALLERGIES, SENSITIVITIES AND REACTIONS
(Non-Life Threatening Conditions)

MEDICINE	FOOD	OTC and/or SUPPLEMENTS	COMPLICATIONS

NOTES

_____

_____

_____

_____

_____

_____'S
LEGAL INFORMATION

ATTORNEY _____

PHONE _____

LIVING WILL YES _____ NO _____

LOCATION _____

DURABLE POWER OF ATTORNEY YES _____ NO _____

LOCATION _____

APPOINTED PERSON _____

_____

_____

NOTES

_____

_____

_____

_____

_____

_____'S
END OF LIFE MEDICAL DECISIONS

It should be understood I am to be consulted and actively involved, to the fullest of my ability, in the decision making process of all life sustaining measures, as well as the discontinuation of all life sustaining measures, as long as I am deemed mentally competent as defined by the State I reside, as determined by two (2) attending physicians.

If at some point in time I no longer meet the definition for mental competency by the State in which I reside as determined by 2 licensed attending physicians, I appoint one of the following people, listed in said order, the authority to make life termination decisions on my behalf:

NAME _____ PHONE _____

RELATIONSHIP _____

NAME _____ PHONE _____

RELATIONSHIP _____

NAME _____ PHONE _____

RELATIONSHIP _____

Must Initial and date page:

_____

_____'S
FUNERAL WISHES

MEMORIAL SERVICE YES _____ No _____

LOCATION _____

_____

CREMATION YES _____ NO _____

PLACE OF INTERNMENT _____

NOTES

_____

_____

_____

_____

_____

EVERYDAY HEROES

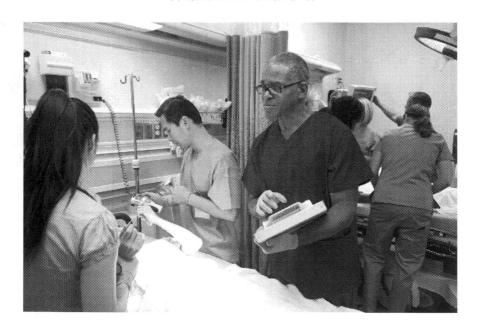

CHILD'S MEDICAL STATS

NAME _____ D/O/B _____

ADDRESS _____

BLOOD TYPE _____ WEIGHT _____

PREFERRED LANGUAGE _____

ORGAN/TISSUE DONOR _____

HISTORY OF RECREATIONAL DRUGS _____

TYPES OF DRUGS _____

ALCOHOL USE _____ CONSUMPTION _____

TOBACCO HISTORY _____

ANY DISABILITY THAT WOULD AFFECT COMMUNICATING
WITH FIRST RESPONDERS? _____

_____

MOTHER'S FULL NAME _____

LAST 4 DIGITS OF SS# _____

FATHER'S FULL NAME _____

LAST 4 DIGITS OF SS# _____

_____'S
I – C – E CONTACTS

NAME _____ PHONE _____

RELATIONSHIP _____

NAME _____ PHONE _____

RELATIONSHIP _____

NAME _____ PHONE _____

RELATIONSHIP _____

NAME _____ PHONE _____

RELATIONSHIP _____

NAME _____ PHONE _____

RELATIONSHIP _____

_____'S
CRITICAL AND LIFE THREATENING CONDITIONS

ALLERGY	MEDICAL ISSUE	REACTION	ANTIDOTE

NOTES

_____

_____

_____

_____

_____

_____'S

CHILDHOOD VACCINATION CHART

VACCINE	1ST DOSE	2ND DOSE	3RD DOSE	4TH DOSE	5TH DOSE
HEPATITIS A					
HEPATITIS B					
D'TaP					
MMR					
PCV					
IPV					

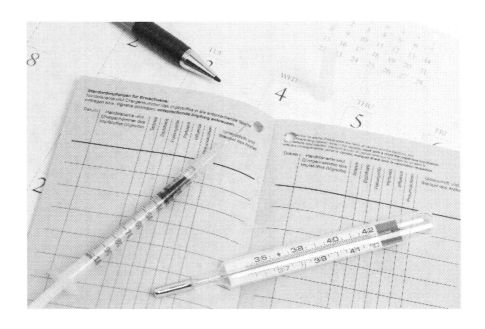

_____'S
INSURANCE INFORMATION

PRIMARY INSURANCE _____

POLICY HOLDER _____

GROUP # _____ ID # _____

SECONDARY INSURANCE _____

POLICY HOLDER _____

GROUP # _____ ID # _____

_____'s PREFERRED HOSPITAL _____

Preferred hospital may be an issue whether it is in network with your primary or secondary insurance. Stating a "preferred" hospital does not guarantee first responders will be able to honor your preference. They will make that decision based on many factors such as the hospital best suited to your medical emergency.

_____'s RELIGIOUS AFFILIATION _____

Religious affiliation is an important issue for those of a faith that limits or prohibits medical treatments such as blood transfusions.

_____'S

DOCTOR'S CONTACT INFORMATION

PRIMARY _____

PHONE _____

ADDRESS _____

SPECIALIST _____

PHONE _____

ADDRESS _____

SPECIALIST _____

PHONE _____

ADDRESS _____

SPECIALIST _____

PHONE _____

ADDRESS _____

SPECIALIST _____

PHONE _____

ADDRESS _____

_____'S

PERSONAL MEDICAL CHART

MEDICATIONS PRESCRIPTIONS & OTC AND DOSES	TREATMENT	HEALTH CARE PROFESSIONAL	PHONE

_____'S

HOSPITALIZATION CHART

REASON FOR HOSPITALIZATION	DATE	TREATMENT	COMPLICATIONS

NOTES

_____

_____

_____

_____

_____

_____'S
SURGERY CHART

PROCEDURE	DATE	TREATMENT	COMPLICATIONS

NOTES

_____

_____

_____

_____

_____

_____'s

ALLERGIES, SENSITIVITIES AND REACTIONS
(Non-Life Threatening Conditions)

MEDICINE	FOOD	OTC and/or SUPPLEMENTS	COMPLICATIONS

NOTES

_____

_____

_____

_____

_____

_____'S
LEGAL INFORMATION

ATTORNEY _____

PHONE _____

LIVING WILL YES _____ NO _____

LOCATION _____

DURABLE POWER OF ATTORNEY YES _____ NO _____

LOCATION _____

APPOINTED PERSON _____

_____

_____

NOTES

_____

_____

_____

_____

_____

_____'S

END OF LIFE MEDICAL DECISIONS

It should be understood I am to be consulted and actively involved, to the fullest of my ability, in the decision making process of all life sustaining measures, as well as the discontinuation of all life sustaining measures, as long as I am deemed mentally competent as defined by the State I reside, as determined by two (2) attending physicians.

If at some point in time I no longer meet the definition for mental competency by the State in which I reside as determined by 2 licensed attending physicians, I appoint one of the following people, listed in said order, the authority to make life termination decisions on my behalf:

NAME _____ PHONE _____

RELATIONSHIP _____

NAME _____ PHONE _____

RELATIONSHIP _____

NAME _____ PHONE _____

RELATIONSHIP _____

Must Initial and date page:

_____

_____'S
FUNERAL WISHES

MEMORIAL SERVICE YES _____ No _____

LOCATION _____

_____

CREMATION YES _____ NO _____

PLACE OF INTERNMENT _____

NOTES

_____

_____

_____

_____

_____

EVERYDAY HEROES

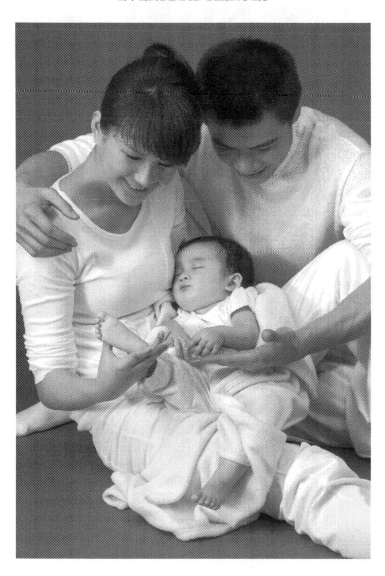

PERSONAL MEDICAL STATS

NAME _____ D/O/B _____

ADDRESS _____

BLOOD TYPE _____ WEIGHT _____

BLOOD PRESSURE _____ PREFERRED LANGUAGE _____

ORGAN/TISSUE DONOR _____

ANY DISABILITY THAT WOULD AFFECT COMMUNICATING
WITH FIRST RESPONDERS? _____

_____

HISTORY OF RECREATIONAL DRUGS _____

TYPES OF DRUGS _____

ALCOHOL USE _____ CONSUMPTION _____

TOBACCO HISTORY _____

NOTES

_____

_____

_____

_____'S
I – C – E CONTACTS

NAME _____ PHONE _____

RELATIONSHIP _____

NAME _____ PHONE _____

RELATIONSHIP _____

NAME _____ PHONE _____

RELATIONSHIP _____

NAME _____ PHONE _____

RELATIONSHIP _____

NAME _____ PHONE _____

RELATIONSHIP _____

_____'S

CRITICAL AND LIFE THREATENING CONDITIONS

ALLERGY	MEDICAL ISSUE	REACTION	ANTIDOTE

NOTES

_____

_____

_____

_____

_____

_____'S
INSURANCE INFORMATION

PRIMARY INSURANCE _____

POLICY HOLDER _____

GROUP # _____ ID # _____

LAST 4 SS# DIGITS _____

SECONDARY INSURANCE _____

POLICY HOLDER _____

GROUP # _____ ID # _____

_____'s PREFERRED HOSPITAL _____

Preferred hospital may be an issue whether it is in network with your primary or secondary insurance. Stating a "preferred" hospital does not guarantee first responders will be able to honor your preference. They will make that decision based on many factors such as the hospital best suited to your medical emergency.

_____'s RELIGIOUS AFFILIATION _____

Religious affiliation is an important issue for those of a faith that limits or prohibits medical treatments such as blood transfusions.

_____'S

DOCTOR'S CONTACT INFORMATION

PRIMARY _____

PHONE _____

ADDRESS _____

SPECIALIST _____

PHONE _____

ADDRESS _____

SPECIALIST _____

PHONE _____

ADDRESS _____

SPECIALIST _____

PHONE _____

ADDRESS _____

SPECIALIST _____

PHONE _____

ADDRESS _____

_____'S

PERSONAL MEDICAL CHART

MEDICATIONS PRESCRIPTIONS & OTC AND DOSES	TREATMENT	HEALTH CARE PROFESSIONAL	PHONE

_____'S
HOSPITALIZATION CHART

REASON FOR HOSPITALIZATION	DATE	TREATMENT	COMPLICATIONS

NOTES

_____

_____

_____

_____

_____

_____'S
SURGERY CHART

PROCEDURE	DATE	TREATMENT	COMPLICATIONS

NOTES

_____

_____

_____

_____

_____

_____'S

ALLERGIES, SENSITIVITIES AND REACTIONS
(Non-Life Threatening Conditions)

MEDICINE	FOOD	OTC and/or SUPPLEMENTS	COMPLICATIONS

NOTES

_____

_____

_____

_____

_____

_____'S
LEGAL INFORMATION

ATTORNEY _____

PHONE _____

LIVING WILL YES _____ NO _____

LOCATION _____

DURABLE POWER OF ATTORNEY YES _____ NO _____

LOCATION _____

APPOINTED PERSON _____

_____

_____

NOTES

_____

_____

_____

_____

_____

_____'S
END OF LIFE MEDICAL DECISIONS

It should be understood I am to be consulted and actively involved, to the fullest of my ability, in the decision making process of all life sustaining measures, as well as the discontinuation of all life sustaining measures, as long as I am deemed mentally competent as defined by the State I reside, as determined by two (2) attending physicians.

If at some point in time I no longer meet the definition for mental competency by the State in which I reside as determined by 2 licensed attending physicians, I appoint one of the following people, listed in said order, the authority to make life termination decisions on my behalf:

NAME _____ PHONE _____

RELATIONSHIP _____

NAME _____ PHONE _____

RELATIONSHIP _____

NAME _____ PHONE _____

RELATIONSHIP _____

Must Initial and date page:

_____

_____'S
FUNERAL WISHES

MEMORIAL SERVICE YES _____ No _____

LOCATION _____

_____

CREMATION YES _____ NO _____

PLACE OF INTERNMENT _____

NOTES

_____

_____

_____

_____

_____

Printed in the United States
By Bookmasters